THE **CRY** OF THE **MILLENNIAL**

WILLIE J. INMAN SR. DD

To order additional copies of this book, contact:
Xlibris
844-714-8691
www.Xlibris.com
Orders@Xlibris.com

All bible scriptures are taken from KJV, public domain.

ISBN: Softcover   978-1-6641-9852-4
          EBook   978-1-6641-9851-7

Print information available on the last page

Rev. date: 11/08/2021

THE **CRY** OF THE MILLENNIAL

Introduction

All throughout history, there has been someone crying. A baby crying for its mother's breast milk, someone losing a loved, one and a vast amount of tragedies that made us cry out to the Lord. There is a new cry going on that many are not hearing. The young adults are crying; however, no one is listening to them. This group of young people are struggling with their identity, not knowing what their real gender is. Some are saying that I am trapped, and I am crying out for help. Another young adult is having problems cohabitating with wanting love, however is afraid to make a total commitment to their partner or vice versa. Also, the credibility of many young folks have been severed toward our older generation because of the examples of many that do not produce what they are saying by the fundamental law of practicing what you are preaching!

This cry has reached out far and wide throughout all countries. Many millennials suffer from depression, oppression, and many have complex personalities. This age expansion has no gender, color, or ethnicity, but all are born between the years of 1981 and 1996. In this book, we will address the different stereotypes that millennials face in everyday life. This will include but not limited to some saying that they have it too easy. We will also speak about how many are leaving home too soon because of lack of guidance and it is causing them to make many mistakes. One idea that stands out is the word "comparison"! Many millennials are comparing themselves to other millennials not being as successful or having a family like their friends.

A great cry is being sent out because of the comparison, and many are getting blamed for the lack of success. Some millennials cannot compare to their upper-class friends that get a full ride to college or because of the bad influences they have been raised with and many coming from broken-family and single-parent homes. They say we cannot compare with them. It's time to break the silence from being ambiguous and fearing to speak about getting blamed for the lack of success among your constituents that were dealt a better hand than you.

We will set the atmosphere as this book draws you into the mind, spirit, and soul of the millennial through seen and unseen things that were forbidden to speak about thirty years ago that is trapped inside of many millennials. It is time for the cry to be heard on the mountaintop. I can hear them saying, "Release me, release me, and let me live my own life!"

Join me on this journey as we explore the complex life of the millennial. We live in an age where we no longer have the strong generational ties that we used to have. Children live thousands of miles from their parents, and older folks are placed in nursing homes. The millennials have to learn as they go or hope they got enough teaching before they left the nest. Let us dive into the heart, mind, and soul of the millennial.

Dedication

I lovingly dedicate this book to my late mother-in-law, Mother Annie Ruth Carter. She went on to be with the good Lord several years ago. She was affectionately known as Butter. She was known to be larger than life itself. Going back to Baxley, Georgia, will never be the same. Butter loved to catch butter or yellow catfish, hence the nickname. Her absence left a big void in our hearts. She has been and will always be sorely missed and never forgotten. I love you, Butter. Continue to rest on with the Lord.

Acknowledgments

The following people assisted with the development of this book. Their work, thoughts, and process were on a strictly-volunteer basis. There would not be a book without them. I am and will forever be grateful. Introducing the names behind the pages:

1. Shera Inman

2. Jeanette Hill

3. Shaqueena Carter

4. Kimberly Inman-Burkhalter

5. Tyrone Bennett

6. Ericka Inman-Bennett

7. Willie Inman Jr.

8. Jashen Hill

Over the course of four years, anyone could get frustrated or tired of hearing about the plans, thoughts, and process of a book. My wife Shera never expressed any frustration with me, the topic, or the process. Jesus puts the right folks in your life to help you accomplish your goals and be your best you. I love you dearly, sweetheart.

Contents

Chapter 1
The Man Cave

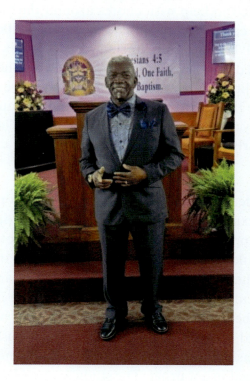

Millennial people today have become much more open-minded about gender roles. It shows up in their attitudes about their words, politics, and sports. They are holding on to traditional views about who does what at home. This area has received minimal changes. Some Gallup polls have shown that among opposite-sex couples, those eighteen to thirty-four, basically millennials and the oldest members of generation Z, were no more likely than older couples to divide household chores equally. Many sociological studies published show a trend in high school seniors when asked about their ideal family arrangement, almost a quarter said it was for the man to work full time and the woman to tend to children. This larger share desired this over any other arrangement. The fact that home life does not look all that different from half a century ago surprises researchers because in most other ways attitudes about gender roles have changed a lot. Millennial men under thirty-five are very supportive of women to pursue careers or political office. Most women get more than millennial men. The younger are much more accepting of people not identifying as either man or a woman.

Many millennial men embrace gender equality but not the concept of house cleaning. Many will not hold their own when asked to help with chores around the home. Many millennials want to split everything 50/50 in most cases, but the millennial man defaults on washing dishes, vacuuming, and dusting the house. He will be more equalitarian when it comes to everything else in the family. However, recent studies based on surveys reported over time show that women now do a little less child care and men do a little more. The main takeaway there is "a little bit." A large gap still remains. Women spend more time a day on housework and an hour more on child care than most millennial men. The disparity affects other aspects of equality. The additional time women spend on domestic labor, particularly related to children, is a leading cause of the gender gaps in pay and promotions at work.

Researchers have different ideas about why the divisions of labor at home have been so slow to change. One of the simplest explanations is that men might be happy to have a partner bringing in another paycheck but not happy to do more chores. Working mothers today spend as much time doing activities with their children as stay-at-home mothers did in the 1970s. Norms about what men are supposed to do also have an effect that researchers say started in childhood, when boys do fewer chores than girls. Masculinity is strongly tied to earning an income and avoiding things that are considered feminine. To be a good millennial man means to be employed. That doesn't mean they don't want to be involved, they do, but the issue is we are pushing up against the prescriptive beliefs about gender. There was a sociology study based on a national survey administered each year to high school seniors published in a journal. The study analyzed data from 1975 to 2015, including over eighty thousand high school seniors.

Young millennial men have grown significantly more open minded over time about women working. The share who preferred having a family with a stay-at-home mother was 28% in 2017, down from 47% in 1979. The share who said that arrangement was unacceptable increased. Also, they have become much more likely to say alternative options are acceptable, like one parent working part time and the other working full time or both working full time. Millennial men whose mothers work full time have been more likely to want a similar arrangement. Those who attend religious services weekly or biweekly or who live in the Southern states have been less open to women working full time. These patterns have not changed over the years. The Gallup surveys on housework were done in 2018, 2006, and 1994 suggest that the opposite-sex couples who were married or living together choose more traditional roles in the home. The gender gap in many chores has shrunk slightly over that period. The millennial men for the most part and the share respondents who say they share tasks equally has been flat.

Millennial males spend less time on average each week consuming traditional TV, only twenty hours, compared to twenty-three hours for millennial females, twenty-eight hours for gen X males and thirty-eight hours for boomer males. However, they make up much of the difference online. This group spends significantly more time per week (two hours, fifteen minutes) than any other demographic watching videos on the Internet.

While these young men are united by age, the group is diverse, and their habits can vary by their ethnicity. African American millennial males, for example, spend significantly more time watching content than millennial men as a whole: These viewers spend nearly thirty-three hours a week with traditional TV and three hours watching videos on the Internet. Hispanic millennial men watch slightly less than the average millennial man, spending an hour less (nineteen hours) on traditional TV and less than two hours watching online videos. Asian American millennial men, on the other hand, spend the most time watching videos on the Internet, almost four hours watching online video but also notably spend the least amount of time watching traditional TV (eleven and half hours).

Millennial men are also heavy music listeners. Of all millennial males in the United States, 88% listen to radio each week, spending more time than their female counterparts tuned in (eleven hours and forty-two minutes versus ten hours and forty-six minutes). They also show more interest in streaming services that are centered to them, such as Spotify and Pandora, than other demographics.

When it comes to social networking, 70% of millennial males were engaged in social networking, while only 38% of older men used social media platforms over the same thirty-day period in the third quarter of 2014. So how did their social profile break down? Of millennial men, 38% used Twitter, 56% downloaded games, 57% downloaded apps, and 51% used a game console, compared with 14%, 24%, 36%, and 23%, respectively, for non-millennial men.

Millennials are more likely than gen X or boomers to hear of what's going on with companies through social media tools, such as Facebook, Twitter, or blogs. They're also more likely to trust the information they learn about a company through social media than information offered elsewhere. Millennials, and males in particular, are less concerned about the increasing amount of personal information that companies capture about their customers these days. While the media has predicted that millennial males are all but impermeable to marketing, data shows that millennial males are not only receptive to marketing, but that they also proactively try to learn more about the companies they hear about or do business with, and their interest is growing.

But just as millennial men consume content differently than millennial women, they also identify with ads differently. So what resonates? "Normal" guys in extreme or exaggerated situations have the strongest effect with this segment, and though humor is a winning characteristic across all audiences, slapstick, edgy, and sarcastic humor resonates highly with younger men. Advertisers in some categories are working overtime to reach this coveted segment, and by tailoring their outreach, they're finding success. For example, within the computers and electronics category, 76% of all impressions served to a campaign aiming to reach millennial males do so successfully, compared with 57% for campaigns aiming to reach the general millennial population.

They don't spend it all in one place! While some companies have found success getting ads to resonate with millennial men, the bigger question marketers want to know is, what makes these trend-setting consumers swipe their credit cards? The answer, it turns out, is frequently electronics. Within the electronics category, millennial males' spending represents more than 10% of total annual spend on electronics among adults. On average, a millennial man shops five times for electronics each year and spends about $77 per trip.

Overall, millennial men's spending across retail categories represents 8% of total adult audiences. That puts them close behind their female counterparts, who account for 9% of total spending across retail categories. Millennial males spend slightly more per shopping trip, but millennial women shop more often. On average, a millennial man spends $2,200 a year in retail, with key categories for the group being mass merchandisers, home improvement, digital apparel/merchandise, electronics, and apparel.

Even though millennial men don't have the same level of discretionary income of other demographics (with a $1 trillion in collective student loan debt, more than a third unemployed, and more than two-thirds at graduation age without bachelor's degrees*), this group is widely considered to be influencers and highly covetable to marketers in their own right. Reaching any demographic has its challenges, but understanding how this young and trendy group consumes content and how receptive they are to marketing messages can help marketers and advertisers focus their efforts and see returns in store. Investing in getting to know your intended audience is as important, or even arguably more important, than the messages themselves.

Finally, millennial males are, in theory, elusive creatures. They're commonly thought of as cord cutters who can't be and don't want to be reached. But many marketers remain eager to connect with this young digitally-savvy group often perceived as innovators, trend starters, and predictors of the next big thing. Millennial males lead the pack, in one way or the other. Today's millennials are the most racially-diverse generation in U.S. history, with nearly 43% identifying as non-white*. They also have spending power. Varying estimates place this group's purchasing power anywhere between $125 billion and $890 billion annually, while some estimates attribute these young shoppers with $200 billion of direct-buying power plus an additional $500 billion in indirect influence based on millennials' powers of persuasion over their baby-boomer parents.

Chapter 2
The Lady of the House

Rushing, gasping for air, thinking uncontrollably, deadlines, work, school, church, kids, marriage, family—then there is nothing. Nothing at all. Have you ever been hurt? Yeah, me too. I know about being hurt all too well. I believe that millennials have experienced hurt on a different level than our ancestors. However, some of us were not taught how to appropriately handle the hurt. Let's talk about it.

Rewind

Here I am, twenty years old, young and free. College is going great. Family is doing fine. Church is going well. I went to church and was in church all the time, but the church was not in me. I was simply in a routine of things. Most millennials around my age, well at least the ones that I was surrounded by when I was younger, had some sense of structure but not enough discipline. Then there I was, singled out. Alone. I always knew that I was different and that things would not work for me unless I did the right thing and practiced critical thinking. Before salvation, I acted saved for the most part because the rule was "If you not saved, you gone act saved." Did I agree? No. Did I obey? Yes. My parents did not mess around. I did not like it at the time, but I deeply appreciate it now. So one day I find myself in a compromising situation. It was one of those situations where you go in for one thing and come out with another. Test results are in—BOOM! You are pregnant, and the lie detector test determined that was the truth, as Maury would say. The world stood still. "Are you okay? Congratulations! Ma'am!? The world started back up, and I was numb. So many thoughts ran through my mind in a matter of what felt like forever, but in reality, it was merely seconds. My world came crashing right before my face all because of one bad decision—sex. You can try to protect yourself all you want, but even protection fails. The only sure way to protect yourself from anything that you may not be ready for at the time is to abstain. I knew what I was doing was wrong and did not plan on it making such a debut, but here I was. What do you do? It was not the fact that I was pregnant. It was the fact that I was pregnant and I knew that I would be on my own. The relationship failed, and it was an abusive one, very verbally/emotionally abusive). You know how there was a ram in the bush? Well, my family turned out to be my ram. My church family did not approve of the decision, but they supported me the entire time. You truly do not know who is in your corner, until the rubber meets the road. Shout out to Mothers Pierce and Harrell. They fought for me, and that is something I will never forget.

Moving Forward

Here I am, twenty-one, just graduated college. Yes, my baby walked across the stage with me literally eight months pregnant. Reality has definitely set in. It troubled me for some time that I placed myself into this situation. However, my immediate family unit helped me through it all. I found myself advocating for any young man or woman who would listen. I had been there and done that. I know what it's like to want something so bad but not need it. I know how hard it can be. However, I wanted them to know their self-value and realize that they are worthy of the best and not just anybody deserves their best. In the midst of it all, I want young people, and people in general, to know that even if you find yourself in a situation such as this one, you can do it! I graduated pregnant with honors (magna cum laude), went back and graduated again as a single parent with honors (summa cum laude), and now getting ready to graduate again as a married woman (not sure about the honors this time, but the point is I made it), and you can do it too! Seek God, follow him, and he will reward you. Was it hard? Yes! Was it and is it still worth it? Yes!

Fast Forward

Have you ever heard the song "I made a vow to the Lord, and I won't take it back"? Well, that is exactly what I did. One day I woke up and said, "Lord, I will not touch (sexually), kiss, or have any form of sex with another man until I get married."

At the time, I was not saved, but I knew that I was going to get saved, so I began to sanctify myself. It was a due process but oh so worth it. While this was happening, it seemed like men came from every direction possible. I prayed hard, fasted, and kept it moving. I had a goal in mind, and I was giving it everything I had to accomplish it. Again, was it easy? No. Was it worth it? Yes. You have to be realistic. I am a realist myself. At that time in life, I would evaluate the situation. It would mainly be about knowing your limits and sticking to staying underneath it. See, I loved men, and the men loved me. So I knew that the enemy was going to try to fight me in that area most definitely. Therefore, I stayed focused, prayed, fasted, and steered clear of compromising situations. Did I live life? Yes indeed. I just lived it more carefully and moved with a purpose. I did all that I could do, but I knew that I was going to need more than just me to win this battle of the flesh. I knew me. The Holy Ghost is a must! So one day I found myself at the altar. I was ready! I gave my life over fully to Jesus! When I say the devil got mad, man, he got big mad. It seems like everything that could happen began to happen. I knew that trials were going to come, but I also knew that Jesus was going to fight for me. I got saved, but you cannot stop there. The Holy Ghost is what you have to attain to be completely covered. It is a keeper if you want to be kept.

Two Minutes of My World

So I met a guy! Fast forward, we are now married with four children. Life is happening right before my eyes! Walk with me. Slow down . . . a little slower . . . that's the pace I'm looking for, but no, it is not happening. I need more time! So much has happened in the ten years of knowing my husband.

We have had ups, downs, thank God for no rock bottoms, and so much more, but I would not trade life with him for anything. He is worth it all! We are worth it all! Marriage is beautiful, contrary to popular belief. This man of mine has me, and he knows it. We have each other! When we made those vows on our wedding day, we made them with a purpose. It is sad to say that many people our age are fleeing from marriage like Joseph did from the women in the Bible. There is nothing wrong with being married and raising a family, you just have to take your time and make sure that you each have an understanding of what is expected and make sure that you are truly compatible. Sex is what people my age think is the big picture. How is the sex, because you are going to be the only person that I am supposed to sleep with because we are married, is a big question. However, my question is, what happens after the sex? Real life is what happens. Sex is an at-the-moment pleasure, but life goes on. Sex can be manipulated into what you want to make it pleasurable in any circumstance between you and your husband or wife, especially if you are in love with each other. That is the beauty of it when you are married for the right reason and to the right mate. Look at us talking about sex freely! Yes! Go, us! We live in a real world, and sex is very much a big part of the millennial world. However, love is the most important thing. If you are in love and will work hard to see the vision through, well, then you are already winning. Quick question for you to think about while you are thinking about marriage: What is more important in your relationship—date night or alone time? Also, while you are thinking about sex, what is more important in your marriage—sex or bills being paid? No, these are not trick questions. Just something to think on what holds the most value. Just know that if you do it right, you can have it all: sex, bills paid on time, date night, and alone time.

In My Closing

Look, I have a sister who says, "Let me go a little further," and when she says that, OMG, that means she has about six or seven more paragraphs of speech left. However, I am not going to go that much further. My dad says that he has "plenty more word, but he is out of time." So let's just use that analogy instead, LOL! In my closing, I am a mother of four, lots of early mornings and late nights, wife of one, and a very hard worker. Although I am *extremely* blessed with a husband who is a wonderful provider, with benefits, might I add, I can and will work for what I want without complaint if I need or want to, and he has no problem with that. I was blessed and raised to attain education. My parents always taught us the importance of education and being able to stand on your own if you had to. You never know what life might bring. So never be so dependent on someone who you would not know what to do if something happened to that someone. Have a plan, millennials, have a plan! My daddy made sure that we could work if we had to or wanted to. That is one thing that the younger generation of millennials struggle with. They want it all right now but will not work hard or work at all to get it. That set of millennials were either raised by someone who was trying to be more of their friend than their parent or they are just spoiled, which is now starting to hurt them. Tomorrow is not promised, no. However, if you are going to live in the moment, make sure you do so wisely because if you do make it to tomorrow, whatever you did yesterday is going to follow you. Just like salvation, your works will follow you! Do I have your attention yet? Good. Basically, I want you to know that as a millennials, we can make it. We are going to go through things. We are not exempt from pain, especially if you plan on making it to heaven. We have to suffer to reign with Jesus! However, it is all in how you handle it. There will be moments of clutching your pearls to say the least. There will be plenty of turning-the-other-cheek, but know that in the end, God has you, and like a good parent, he does not play about his children! Can I get an Amen? No? Well, that is okay because I brought my help with me, as my dad would say! We millennials are not as bad as some make us out to be. It all depends on the raising, training, relationship with God, and so forth. For those who will take teaching, teach them. For those who will take help, help them. For those who will listen, talk to them. You see where I am headed with this, right? Do not just talk about them, help them. Not only is the struggle real, but the cry is also, hence the cry of the millennial. Will there be one? Okay, seriously this time, I am about to close, even though I am just getting warmed up. This is not my book, just a chapter in a book, so I am going to save the rest for later. Hopefully, I have given you much to think about in a positive manner! As I say every day at work, thank you so much for your patience, have a great day!

Chapter 3
The Silent Scream

In recent years, millennials have been called the burnout generation. Whether it is school, work, family life, or the social arena, the generation is tormented by adversity. According to the World Health Organization, more than 40% of people are affected by depression globally and, in recent decades, has reached epidemic proportions. The millennial generation is right in the middle of it all. Having survived through multiple economic recessions, crippling student loan debt, and the COVID-19 pandemic, among other things, it is impossible not to see how this issue would adversely affect an entire generation.

According to a study conducted by Blue Cross Blue Shield from 2014 to 2017, major depression increased 31%. Why? The main reason millennials give when asked why they do not seek help is that they are afraid of being rejected. We all have a need to belong and crave some sort of solidarity in our emotional experiences. It is this need for acceptance that becomes destabilized when we get rejected. And it is that sense of detachment that leaves us with added emotional pain. In some cultures, depression is a weakness, and it is dismissed and ignored. This results in feelings of abandonment that can eventually turn into resentment and lead to bitterness.

There are many different types of depression, and they can all present in a plethora of ways. Manic (bipolar disorder), antenatal, postnatal/postpartum, seasonal affective disorder (SAD), melancholia, and clinical are all different types of depression. Irritability, sleep disturbances, anxiety, feelings of worthlessness, extreme fatigue, frequent suicidal thoughts, and mania are examples of the many symptoms one may discern in a depressed person.

These feelings can lead to thoughts of self-harm, which can end in suicide. According to a study conducted by Solera Mental Health, self-harm rates are up to 14% in millennials. Though by outward appearances they may seem to be in the prime of their lives, research shows that millennials are more likely to die prematurely from suicide than previous generations. In a report by public health groups Trust for America's Health and Well Being Trust, millennials saw a 35% increase in deaths by suicide from 2007 to 2017. Suicide is the second leading cause of death for the millennial generation. According to that same study, millennials, compared to other generations, have the highest rate of poverty, are often less likely to own a home, and in the United States, have the highest number of single-mother households. Speaking of millennial women, they are 20% less healthy than their male counterparts.

This is a lot to take in, right? Well, do not fret because there is hope! So even if you find yourself thinking these feelings and thoughts apply, it is best to seek a medical professional's advice. If you or someone you know are having thoughts of suicide, please call your doctor or mental health professional, call a suicide hotline number, reach out to a friend or loved one, or contact someone in your faith community.

The millennial generation, as a whole, takes mental health very seriously. Many of them grew up in toxic homes dealing with verbal, physical, and mental abuse. Most of which was swept under the rug for the sake of "keeping an image." For those millennials who grew up in religious circles, it seems to have been double jeopardy, knowing what went on at your home, but subsequently watching your guardian(s) act as if nothing was wrong while in the presence of their fellow churchgoers, not realizing that the others also knew but were not doing anything to help the situation, just quietly spectating on the sidelines. Many describe this as church hurt.

I believe this is the reason so many millennials are leaving the church. They've grown up watching the people who were supposed to be living the life the word of God tells us to do the exact opposite. They were told "to do as I say, but not as I do," as if their lifestyle was Godly and they would somehow make it into heaven while disobeying the very word they preached. It makes sense to be conflicted and want to separate because how could God overlook all of those things for the people in charge, but condemn me to hell if I did the same things? As the millennials say, it's giving contradictory behavior.

God has never and will never change! He cannot be a different God for each generation. It is not in his nature to change. The millennial generation is looking for God's people to not only preach the word but to live it also—book, chapter, verse. The church has been riddled with scandals in the last few decades. Not just the megachurches either. Our local churches have endured scandals, and some kept on going with little to no reprehension. It is no wonder the younger generations take the church as a joke in this day and age.

If the church would turn away from our wicked ways and show ourselves worthy of leading his people, we could begin to win back some of the lost and damaged souls. Some of which we are directly responsible for. I believe once the church redeems itself and begins to align itself back with the word of God, we can break the cycle of this depressive spirit that has tried to take our future generations out of the church.

To do this, we must first hold ourselves, especially those in leadership, accountable for the damage that we have caused living in our flesh. Next comes the acknowledgment of the fact that some of us were a bad example. We must then rectify all those bad decisions we made and walk the line from then on. The only way for the millennials to begin to trust the church again is by showing them that we can and will live right before them and in the eyesight of God at all times. God will do the rest as long as we uphold our part of being the example they can follow.

Finally, this is the scream that is not heard because it is silent. Depression, oppression, and suicide cry out in the millennial community on a daily basis. My question is, who is listening to all these signs from the younger generation? They are so consumed with all the negativity that their life has drowned them in that they cannot help their own children to advance in life. Many millennials are divorcing in record numbers because they just don't know how to cope with the changes that life forces on you. Who can hear their scream? Help is available for all your inter needs.

Chapter 4
Get Out of the Cycle

Let's be honest: We all can think of two or three bad habits that we need to shake. Whether we know it or not, bad habits can deter us from reaching our goals and aspirations. They are a stumbling block and serve no other purpose than to keep us locked in an unhealthy cycle. To reach our goals and aspirations, we must identify the bad habits and break the cycle. To begin the journey towards freedom, we must identify the problem by admitting that you have one. Until we can come to terms with the fact that we have a problem, we cannot begin the steps to rectify the situation. Also, admitting the problem allows us to open up to someone we can trust and confide in to help us move forward. Seeking help is the second part of this process and very important. After admitting the problem to ourselves and then to someone else, we are ready to set up a plan of attack to rid ourselves of ugly habits.

This person should be someone you admire and look up to and sets a positive example to anyone who is around them. Most people find licensed therapists, ministers, pastors, counselors, or trusted friends to talk with about whatever issue is plaguing their lives. Now that we have a confidant, we have to establish some boundaries about who we allow into our space. I've learned that some people are cool to be around but negative role models. You have to realize who in your life feeds into bad behavior and who feeds into positivity. The bad role models could be triggers for the bad habits that you wish to end. If you continue to allow their negativity around all the progress that you are accomplishing with your confidant, then they will only take you backwards. Don't be afraid to cut ties with things and people that incite bad behavior.

It's time for you to take control of your life. No longer will you make bad decisions that you didn't even think through. You are not a product of your past. Don't ever let anyone make you feel like you are less because of a decision or action that you made. Every day is a new start and full of wonderful possibilities! God gives us brand-new mercies every day! Remember, no one said that you have to be perfect. But you should strive to be better every day! Consistency is also another step in the process. If we are not consistent in what is required to keep the bad cycles broken, then we are sure to fall back into them eventually. You should check in with your confidant every month or when your schedules will allow.

Your confidant is your accountability partner. Always be honest with them so they can give you the best help possible. Sometimes consistency can even involve picking up new healthy and positive hobbies, like riding horses, bicycling, playing basketball, football, golf, learning a musical instrument, etc. When we fill our free time with things to do, then we have less time to wonder about old habits. Also, seeking and surrounding yourself with positive thinkers is a great way to fill your time. Your mental health is the last and most important part of this process. You have to know who you are and what great things you are capable of! You should wake every morning and say, "I am somebody who is great and awesome, and today is going to be terrific!" It's all about your outlook.

Finally, millennials are doing something right. Can we start talking about how millennials are breaking cycles of intergenerational pain?

Millennials have the same number of sexual partners as baby boomers, but they're not getting married at the same rates or having children.

It's one of the greatest clichés, no matter which time you look at. The older generation finds the younger generation to be "too much," too forward, too outlandish, and too irresponsible. Somehow that younger generation always manages to grow up and step into that same role and repeat the same critique of the next generation. There's simply no clash quite like the millennials and boomers. Boomers are apparently shocked by the results of their own parenting skills. Millennials are resentful and bitter, expressing dismay at the economy they're expected to survive in and showing a greater awareness of trauma and mental health than any previous generation.

Is there some justification for the (at times) self-entitled behavior boomers see in millennials? The divorce rate and the decline of a close family unit might just play a part in the collective issues displayed by gen Y.

Boomers happily jump in and out of marriage. Baby boomers were the first adults to have access to safe and reliable contraception. They're also the first batch of fully-fledged adults to have legal access to safe clinical abortions. Does this mean they had a whole lot more sex than previous generations? It certainly does. But that doesn't mean they stopped getting married. Marriage was still a social norm that was seen as the gateway into adulthood—you had to have engaged in matrimony to truly be an adult. Now that it was possible to separate sex from starting a family, men and women wanted to break out of their often mundane marriages. There was a slightly-weird coexistence between marriage and sexual liberty, and that resulted in a seriously catastrophic divorce rate. Not necessarily catastrophic for the boomers. From the millennials' perspective, their parents were #livingtheirbestlife. The loss of the family unit, the dividing of resources between couples, and the emotional havoc that goes with divorce became an epidemic in the lives of young millennials.

Millennials are no longer seeing marriage as the portal to anything. In fact, this generation is more resistant to calls of matrimonial life than any other. They're getting married much later and having fewer children. Interestingly, they're not having that much more sex than boomers. Boomer women averaged ten partners in their lives, while men averaged twelve. This is an increase from their predecessors (yup, grandma wasn't all that innocent either), and millennial numbers have reached a steady 10.8 average sexual partners among men and women (collectively).

Does this mean that millennials are getting it right, they're having sex responsibly without bringing kids into the mix and complicating matters? Who knows? Gen Z, those born after 1995, are set to have the most sex, statistically, averaging 5.6 sexual partners already this early in their lives.

Last, you are the key to breaking the cycle that may have followed you most of your life. It may have even been generational. But you have the power to say enough is enough! Nothing is impossible if you put your mind to it. The bad cycle that you have broken is now a testimony for someone who may be struggling with the same thing you may have fought for years. All your hard work and persistence was for them to someday look at your situation and be strengthened and empowered. From now on, no matter what position you find yourself in, remember, God is able, and he can and will deliver!

Chapter 5
The Modern-Day Witness

While the world grows more and more spiritually immoral to the will and way of God, the redemptive role of the church for a dying world cannot be any clearer. Because times have changed, the church's strategy to draw the millennial generation back to the church began to change to trendy worship, flashy styles, and more nontraditional programs. Much to their surprise, millennials are still leaving the church quicker now than any other generation ever before. Why?

The expression "Build it and they will come" can be misleading when the millennial comes! The question that should be asked is, what will make them stay? For he was looking for the city which has foundations, whose architect and builder is God, Hebrews 11:10. This generation, although not as experienced as their predecessors, wants the same thing any other person is looking for when coming to church, to know God, of course, and to have an authentic experience and follow credible leadership.

Millennials are rather intelligent and can smell a phony a mile away or even a click away. Social media and television have made immoral behavior among spiritual leaders more apparent today. Although they know this to be true, they are not looking for imperfections in the church. Instead, they are looking for God's delivering power to reach far past what can be seen with the natural senses. For too long have this generation's gifts been used in the church without seeing life-changing benefits in their own life.

The saying "Practice what you preach!" is very true. Holiness is a lifestyle and not a fad. It can't be put on or taken off like the clothes we wear. To keep the interest of this unique group of people, the church has got to come off the surface with the word of God and allow biblical truths to be taught in a way that transcend primary Sunday school lessons and become relevant in a manner that a millennial can apply them in their everyday life. A puree diet is filling for a baby if it has no teeth. Once he or she grows teeth and discovers that milk and a puree diet are not the only items on the menu, they are ready to move to bigger and better things. Millennials feel the same way. Take the training wheels off! Millennials are looking for leadership in the church that can answer the questions that no one wants to answer. For example: What's wrong with fornication? Where is it in the Bible? They may be the most inquisitive generation yet. This sometimes can be mistaken as being prying or maybe even pushy. However, what some see as weakness is this generation's strongest quality. Church, it's time to keep it real! Time and seasons in our lives will change, but holiness should stay the same. As long as we're *in* the world and not *of* the world, the millennial will see that we serve an authentic and credible God.

Among U.S. millennials who are practicing Christians, 47% agree "it is wrong to share one's personal beliefs with someone of a different faith in hopes that they will one day share the same faith," according to research by the Special Group released February 5.

Millennials' level of agreement with that statement was higher than among generation X (27%), baby boomers (19%) and elders (20%). Still, a full 96% of millennial Christians in the United States believe part of their faith is "being a witness about Jesus," Special Group reported.

About 94% say, "The best thing that could ever happen to someone is for them to come to know Jesus."

Special Group defined millennials as individuals born between 1984 and 1998 (ages twenty-one to thirty-five). Millennial Christians believe that evangelism is wrong, came in spite of high self-confidence about their witnessing abilities. Special Group reported 86% of millennials said they know how to respond "when someone raises questions about faith," and 73% said they are "gifted at sharing their faith."

Smith Jenkins, a former Southern Baptist convention member, said believers should "be careful not to hit the panic button over a single answer to a survey" because millennial believers "have the potential to have a huge impact for Jesus. I have met so many who are sold out to Jesus and serious about having an impact for him.

"More than anything, this report should cause us to look at our churches and ask, 'What are we teaching our young people? Are we effectively passing the faith baton to the next generation?' In most cases, the answer is 'We need to do better,'" Hunt said.

Smith, likewise, cautioned against painting "an entire generation with a broad brush when we see studies like the Special Group one." Yet cultural and church-related trends "have played a role in producing a spirit of fear and timidity about evangelism among millennials."

"Today's culture seduces this generation with a thought process that says that all faiths are equal," said Smith, an evangelist based in Georgia. "Today's philosophy says that it doesn't matter what you believe or don't believe, and anyone who says it does matter must be a bigot." Within churches, Smith said, part of the failure to disciple millennials is not exposing them "to the huge multitude of Christian youth" around the world "who once were Muslim, Hindu, Buddhist, Sikh, and atheist" and have come to Christ through "great moves of the Spirit of God" in "places like China, Iran, and India. Global millennial believers are "on fire" for Christ, Smith said.

U.S. millennials' lack of exposure to global Christians is "paradoxical because millennials are a generation that is multicultural, multinational, and multi-ethnic," Smith said. "We need to build networks through social media, the Internet, and communication technology that enable this generation to rub shoulders with those who have the smoke of heaven in their hearts. Lifeway Research's 2018 State of Theology survey, sponsored by Ligonier Ministries, found 90% of eighteen-to thirty-four-year-old evangelicals say it is "very important for me personally to encourage non-Christians to trust Jesus Christ as their Savior."

Lifeway Research's survey did not ask about millennials' practice of personal evangelism and began cleanup work in Marshalltown, Iowa, following a devastating tornado July 19. A disaster relief team arrived Tuesday to set up an incident command at Iglesias Kairos in Marshalltown. Chainsaw teams from Iowa have dispersed throughout the city to clear debris. An SBDR feeding team has prepared meals for recovery workers in the area.

"It looks like a war zone to tell you the truth. "When you go downtown, you'll see a lot of glass and brick everywhere. "On the east part of town, there are about ten blocks that are very heavily hit. There's really not many trees standing. A lot of those homes aren't livable. This town was devastated and needed many millennial and others to come help speak and comfort folks that had lost everything.

The EF-3 tornado injured at least 235 people in the town of twenty-seven thousand. It was estimated that at least one hundred homes were destroyed. Many more homes will take substantial work before people can return to live in them. Also, it was believed that it would take months, if not years, for Marshalltown to rebuild. Some of the worst damage in Marshalltown came to the town's courthouse and the brick buildings in the town square. In recent years, officials and property owners had slowly worked to revamp the buildings, many of which are now destroyed. Many leaders of the Marshalltown Central Business District estimate that the city had spent $50 million in building renovations since 2002. A dozen or more tornadoes hit Central Iowa last Thursday, according to the National Weather Service. The two biggest tornadoes, both rated EF-3, hit Marshalltown and Pella, with peak winds of 144 mph.

Millennial chaplains were in Marshalltown to provide support and counsel to residents impacted by the tornado. Many millennials prayed that the SBDR response will provide volunteers opportunities to share the gospel. "The number one goal with disaster relief is to earn the right to share the gospel, "We work with those impacted. We treat them with respect. We pray with them. When they ask the question, 'What makes you do this for no charge?' That's when you've earned the right to share The Marshalltown tornado comes on the heels of the SBDR response to flooding in Des Moines, Iowa, where teams wrapped up work last week. Eight people came to faith in the last week during SBDR efforts in the capital city.

Finally, many millennials that are a part of the Christian domain were here to pray for Marshalltown and the rest of Central Iowa. Pray for all the people who live here. A lot of millennials lost their homes. They lost their cars. They lost their jobs. There is a lot of a need here. The last thirty years have left many millennials with some baggage. The fire-breathing model of engagement practiced by some leaders of the "moral majority" left many millennials with a bad taste in their mouth. The disillusioned and confused millennial masses include many young pastors and scholars who find their identity in the vibrant movement of the last decade (like the *New York Times*, you may have just heard of it). Young Christian leaders today often express a desire to distance themselves from the moral majority. This is a partly helpful and partly unhelpful response to their heritage. It is helpful because it means that many young millennial church planters and pastors and thinkers will avoid reducing the faith to a policy position. They will focus on making friendships with people not like them and living another way of life. The church will be the listening church, a spiritual body of believers that gathers to hear the lion of the scripture roar from his word each week.

This response is unhelpful because young Christian leaders might forget that the church must also be the speaking church. Many millennial leaders understand the dire need for evangelization of lost friends, but fewer grasp the importance of public square witnessing. Few of the millennials will emulate the moral majority at its apex, but we also must recognize that, in their imperfect way, various figures of this group spoke courageously on behalf of the unborn, the natural family, and the moral fabric of the nation. There was real bravery and real sacrifice in this witness. It came at a real cost in a culture and society that now reads any attempt, however noble, to intervene in others' lives as hostile and injurious.

Unlike the moral majority, many millennials are quiet as a church mouse on public square issues, save for a vocal rejection of past tactics. A church inspired by the gospel, aware of its claim on all of life and in tune with a historic tradition of figures like Augustine and Colson, cannot content itself with exquisitely-calibrated public neutrality. Neither can it accept the velvet muzzle its opponents offer. It cannot dance like a celebrity on his way back to the list when a confused church member asks for guidance on cultural questions of grave import.

Chapter 6
Playing Like a Child (Media)

Social media plays a very important role in today's society of accessibility. Social media is a way that many people socialize, as well as communicate, without having any physical interactions. In the world we live in today, it is almost impossible not to be a part of the social media world. Practically, we all communicate with at least one social media platform in our day-to-day lives. Businesses, along with other corporations, are expanding their social interactions daily. Not only that, but they are also rapidly reconstructing their businesses upon social technology. According to Oberlo, social media statistics from 2019 show that there are 3.5 billion social media users worldwide and that 90.4% of millennials are within that billion. For some, that may mean a few times a day, and for others, a few days out of the week. Either way, no matter how much time you spend on social media, you still contribute to it in some type of way. Social media has almost become like an addiction for some. By addiction, when one wakes up in the morning, do one go straight to their phone? If so, that person might have a serious problem. There is a difference between checking the time and turning off an alarm. On the other hand, if one has to scroll through Facebook, Instagram, Twitter, or any other preferable app before getting out of bed, one might be slightly addicted.

Some millennials tend to rely on social media for their daily function of life, which is the worst thing a person can do. Because of the impact social media has had on the millennial generation, many things are not as disclosed as they used to be. One of the most atrocious effects social media can have on one is the habit of comparison. Comparing your life to someone else's is a huge issue. For example, Person A might see Person B post the celebration of just signing a major record deal. Person A has been waiting for what seems like forever to do the same thing. Just because Person B received his break sooner than Person A does not mean Person A will not achieve their own personal goals and aspirations. Everyone has their own path to take, and there is nothing you can do about that. It is critical to understand that everyone has separate journeys and talents that God has blessed every individual. Instead of trying to hate and figure out why a person has encountered their blessing before first, one should be congratulating that person. This helps with a person's confidence; nobody understands what a person has to experience to get their blessing. Also, the people who are receiving their breakthrough might be able to give relatable advice that will help along someone's journey. Possibly, that person could be next, just never know.

It is almost like what is presented to be viewed is only a small portion of what their life actually consists of. As a viewer on the outside looking in, one could see wealth, happiness, and longevity, but in reality, it is turmoil. This is where a lot of today's millennials have gone wrong. A person would rather stunt and show off on what seems to be the best life, rather than actually trying to pursue a life of stability. Many millennials find themselves struggling so much, unto the point where it is deemed as unproblematic. It has become so common that a huge number sees it as the new normal. Why do millennials feel that it is better to tear down rather than to embrace? Truth be told, everyone comes from different backgrounds, nationalities, ethnicities, and cultures. Not only that, but we're all a part of the makeup of this earth. God's creation is set upon diversity. Until we realize that we all play different roles here on earth, we are never going to progress.

Social media can either be a free-time occupier or a competitive life challenge. Not everyone comes from the same place in life. For some, buying their own pair of shoes with money they have earned is an accomplishment, while for others, it is given to them as a spoiled privilege. Why is it that millennials feel like taking their personal business to social media is something that is cool or trendy? Do not get confused, not all millennials have this habit, but a big majority does. Social media is not a platform to tell friends and family that one's baby daddy cheated with one's best friend. Everyone has seen posts like that over a million times. Nothing positive comes from disclosing your personal life like that. The results from having an open life like that will bring nosy users and drama in the comment section and in real life. Millennials seriously need to do better as a generation and actually think critically about what they are doing when they type their problems for the world to see, especially living in a world where people would rather help push you down than pick you up. One main problem is that they seek the validation of others. For example, Facebook. Everyone knows about Facebook. When the app first began, it only had one reaction, which was a like. As of 2020, users now have the choice of six different reaction buttons. Those reactions include like, love, wow, sad, and angry. Why in the world does the world need a selection of reactions? The answer once again is validated. Gen Y has become so caught up on opinions and what others have to say rather than their own thoughts and feelings. Why does it matter so much? Is it society that has us focused on approvals, or could it be a personal thing? Either way, the sad part about it is that the world allows a reaction to depict their feelings. If one has a like rather than a love, or a sad instead of a ha-ha, it can be expressed. Things like this lead to self-esteem issues and even depression. It should not matter how many nor what kind of reactions do you get. This is why one should not allow social media to become habitual in their life, or it could possibly become unhealthy for a person in numerous ways. It is all unhealthy when it is actually thought about.

Have you ever wondered why so many millennial relationships are going downhill? When it comes to relationships, it takes the effort of both companions. Social media has the new trend of setting requirements on the basis of how a relationship should go. For example, the phrase "relationship goals." What exactly does that mean? Is it the actual goals that you want in a relationship, or is it the goals of someone else's? Nothing is wrong with having the same goals as others, but make sure they are based on each other and not big-time celebrities.

Overall, social media has made a huge impact on generation Y. You can choose to view it negatively or positively. The challenge for millennials to do should be to remove all the negative and increase the positive from all aspects. Detox yourself from social media, and take some time to isolate yourself. Take a break from the opinions, approvals, and rejections of others to find yourself. The change can only begin once you take the necessary steps to do so. Ask yourself this question today! How has social media impacted my life? The word "addiction" brings to mind alcohol and drugs. Yet over the past twenty years, a new type of addiction has emerged: addiction to social media. It may not cause physical harm, such as those caused by tobacco and alcohol, but it has the potential to cause long-term damage to our emotions, behavior, and relationships. While the older generation, those born in the baby-boom period shortly after World War 2, had alcohol and drugs as their vice, the younger generation, the so-called millennials, have social media as theirs. The millennials, born between 1984 and 2005, have embraced the digital age, using technology to relax and interact with others. Social media is a big deal for them; it is a lifeline to the outside world.

Although people of all ages use social media, it is more harmful for younger users than it is for older people. Addiction may seem a bit of a strong word to use in the context of social media, but addiction refers to any behavior that is pleasurable and is the only reason to get through the day. Everything else pales into insignificance. Millennials may not get liver damage or lung cancer from social media, but it can be damaging, nonetheless. The harm lies in their change in behavior. Their addiction means spending an increasing amount of time online to produce the same pleasurable effect, and it means social media is the main activity they engage in above all others. It also means taking away attention from other tasks, experiencing unpleasant feelings from reducing or stopping interaction with social media and restarting the activity very soon after stopping completely.

We should also be concerned about the effect of social media on sleep and doing less "offline," such as making time for work responsibilities and direct face-to-face social interaction. It has also been linked to depression and loneliness, both of which may be the cause or the effect of social media addiction. Millennials report compulsively checking social network profiles and updates. They can make riskier decisions and be open to online exploitation. They often mistakenly believe that, if things go wrong, they will get help from their online community, even if this community consists of relative strangers.

Millennials are more narcissistic than previous generations. Most of us rely partly on the ability to reflect on our thinking, feeling, and behaving to form our own self-image. The problem with social media is that self-image relies mainly on others and their opinions. A recent study found higher narcissism (an exaggerated self-image of intelligence, academic reputation, or attractiveness) in millennial college students compared with previous generations. This does not bode well for a society where self-reflection is key to making informed and balanced decisions.

The digital age has changed the nature of addictions in millennials who have replaced one maladaptive behavior with another. Social media certainly looks as if it has replaced alcohol as a way of social interaction with others. It is perhaps no surprise that, over the past ten years, there has been a 20% rise in the proportion of sixteen- to twenty-four-year-olds. Ten years ago, it was 17%. It is now 24%. Spending time online now seems more desirable than spending time in a pub with friends.

There is no recognized treatment for social media addiction. Although we are starting to become aware of the problem, there is no classification of social media addiction as a mental disorder in the same way as substance misuse. If we want this to happen, there needs to be a clearer definition of the symptoms and progression over time. We will need to answer some key questions, such as does it run in families? Are there blood tests that can distinguish it from other mental disorders? And will it respond to drugs or psychological therapies? We still have more questions than answers.

Demographic data is a key building block in defining your target audiences on social media. Generational nuances have a huge impact on how people interact with your brand, from the awareness stage all the way on to advocacy. The Harris Poll, on behalf of Sprout Social, surveyed over one thousand U.S. consumers to understand how they use social media today, and how they plan on using it in the future. To investigate how age plays a role in these decisions, we broke down the data by the following generations:

- Generation Z (survey respondents ages 18–24)
- Millennials (survey respondents ages 25–40)
- Generation X (survey respondents ages 41–56)
- Baby Boomers (survey respondents ages 57–74)

The results shed light on several distinctions in social media use by generation. Although trends do change based on age, one thing is for certain: Every generation increased their social media use over the past year. As social adoption surges across all age groups, understanding how different generations use social media is more important than ever. This guide outlines everything you need to know about the social media behaviors and expectations of each generation so you can tailor your efforts for maximum impact.

Chapter 7
The House Prophet

The test of a prophet starts at birth. According to scripture, men born of a woman are but a few days and are full of trouble. Through my own life, my tests started in elementary school being bullied because I loved the Lord. Coming up through fifth grade, I gave my life to Christ and promised I'd serve Jesus 'til I die. Can you believe that a fifth-grade student committed their life to Christ? All the while, God was using me, and I didn't even know it. I would preach on the bus, and folks would get mad and curse me and my God. Many things happened as a result, especially as I get older, that would test and try my vow to God. While I was in middle school up to high school, there was always a man by the name of Mr. Eldridge who looked out for me. He was placed there by God, and he was a preacher. He came from the old-school holiness church. He'd always keep an eye on me. When the tests started rolling in, he always knew when I was at a breaking point because he would look in his rearview mirror and look me in the eyes and shake his head.

Even through middle and high school, I was tried and tested to see if I'd stand. I had to sacrifice some things for him to see if I would stand! That's just a little piece of my story coming up, but everybody's test is different, and he tailors it to what you specifically have to do as a prophet. The problem with our generation, millennials, is that we have this idea that we can effectively operate with no training. We have young millennial prophets who are saved, sanctified, and full of the Holy Ghost and that with fire *but* no training, and this is where the rubber meets the highway. Think about it like the karate kid. Everyone must have a teacher. You cannot teach yourself something that you've never done and be as effective as possible. For example, Apostle Paul and Timothy, Elisha and Elijah, Moses and Joshua, and the list goes on. They all had a sensei. Their gifts that they had coupled with the knowledge that they learned helped them become seasoned in what they were doing. Simply put, it takes time! Do not rush the process. Let God season you through your leader.

There are two types of millennial prophets: One is a male, and the other is a female. They work in most of the nine gifts of the spirit. They see, feel, and hear things from Jesus. Also, I think millennials are amazing, and I am very excited about this generation! A lot has been said negatively about them, and a lot of the concerns are facts, but I know the Lord has a great plan for them. I'm excited about a generation that's equipped with information at their fingertips because I believe, at some point, they will realize just because it is out there does not mean it is accurate. Millennials will have to learn how to discern truth, and as they seek the truth, they will find him. I know that Jesus is the only way, so they will find out the truth if they're looking for it.

With regard to millennial prophets, one of the biggest obstacles we push up against is the pace at which culture runs. We can "connect" so easily these days, whether through social media or the Internet. The average Instagram user will scroll once every one to two seconds, meaning to grab the attention of people these days, you have to do it quickly, and although we are the most "connected," we are the most emotionally-disconnected generation. Many millennials are virtually connected but not personally connected to anything real or tangible. For this generation to thrive, they need to intentionally slow down. This generation has formed unhealthy habits: Silence, stillness, and solitude have been weeded out because we have the ability to be fed by information or some kind of interest at all times.

This is the challenge: To connect with God is not going to take one second, it requires being silent, alone, and still. Rest is almost countercultural, but it is vital for our spiritual, physical, and emotional health. The prophets need to be rooted and grounded in the word and to not be swayed by the wind of their culture, to move at the pace of God and not the pace of the on-demand culture. They'll have to push back against the demand of production and learn that abiding in his presence daily is the most productive.

What is your prophetic push in life?

"And by a prophet, the LORD brought Israel out of Egypt and by a prophet was he preserved." (Hosea 12:13, KJV)

OBJECTIVE of the Millennial Prophet

Don't create a theology out of your pain to teach others that things have to happen your way because you're justifying your hurt or error.

***1. Some will remain only a shepherd until there is a prophetical push to another level. (1 Samuel 16:1–3)

There must be a personal hunger to initiate the birthing of your next *push* to another level.

> ¹And the LORD said unto Samuel, How long wilt thou mourn for Saul, seeing I have rejected him from reigning over Israel? Fill thine horn with oil, and go, I will send thee to Jesse the Bethlehemite: for I have provided me a king among his sons.
>
> ²And Samuel said, how can I go? If Saul hear [it], he will kill me. And the LORD said, Take a heifer with thee, and say, I am come to sacrifice to the LORD.
>
> ³And call Jesse to the sacrifice, and I will shew thee what thou shalt do: and thou shalt anoint unto me [him] whom I name unto thee. (1 Samuel 16:1–3, KJV)

***2. You don't always get all of your instructions at the time of your anointing, wait for the word. (1 Samuel 16:11–13)

After Samuel anointed David, David returned to the sheep, but the spirit of the Lord was upon him from that day and forward.

¹¹And Samuel said unto Jesse, Are here all [thy] children? And he said, there remained yet the youngest, and, behold, he keepeth the sheep. And Samuel said unto Jesse, Send and fetch him: for we will not sit down till he comes hither.

¹²And he sent, and brought him in. Now he [was] ruddy, [and] withal of a beautiful countenance, and goodly to look to. And the LORD said, Arise, anoint him: for this [is] he.

¹³Then Samuel took the horn of oil, and anointed him in the midst of his brethren: and the Spirit of the LORD came upon David from that day forward. So Samuel rose up, and went to Ramah. (1 Samuel 16:11–13, KJV)

***3. Being an armor-bearer is only part of your anointing. You were anointed to be the king. (1 Samuel 16:18–23)

Don't become complacent being an armor-bearer. Learn the lessons of being an armor-bearer, but your hunger is going to create your next *push*, not you.

¹⁸Then answered one of the servants, and said, Behold, I have seen a son of Jesse the Bethlehemite, [that is] cunning in playing, and a mighty valiant man, and a man of war, and prudent in matters, and a comely person, and the LORD [is] with him.

¹⁹Wherefore Saul sent messengers unto Jesse, and said, Send me David thy son, which [is] with the sheep.

²⁰And Jesse took an ass [laden] with bread, and a bottle of wine, and a kid, and sent [them] by David his son unto Saul.

²¹And David came to Saul, and stood before him: and he loved him greatly; and he became his armor-bearer.

²²And Saul sent to Jesse, saying, Let David, I pray thee, stand before me; for he hath found favor in my sight.

²³And it came to pass, when the [evil] spirit from God was upon Saul, that David took a harp, and played with his hand: so Saul was refreshed, and was well, and the evil spirit departed from him. (1 Samuel 16:18–23, KJV)

***4. Your next call is not about cheeses, it's always been about purpose. (1 Samuel 17:17–23)

It is easy to become complacent with your walk if you think all there is to your walk is only delivering cheeses.

¹⁷And Jesse said unto David his son, Take now for thy brethren an ephah of this parched [corn], and these ten loaves, and run to the camp to thy brethren;

¹⁸And carry these ten cheeses unto the captain of [their] thousand, and look how thy brethren fare, and take their pledge.

¹⁹Now Saul, and they, and all the men of Israel, [were] in the valley of Elah, fighting with the Philistines.

²⁰And David rose up early in the morning, and left the sheep with a keeper, and took, and went, as Jesse had commanded him; and he came to the trench, as the host was going forth to the fight, and shouted for the battle.

²¹For Israel and the Philistines had put the battle in array, army against army.

²²And David left his carriage in the hand of the keeper of the carriage, and ran into the army, and came and saluted his brethren.

²³And as he talked with them, behold, there came up the champion, the Philistine of Gath, Goliath by name, out of the armies of the Philistines, and spake according to the same words: and David heard [them]. (1 Samuel 17:17–23)

In summary, the millennial prophet is one who will operate and teach about the millennial reign of Christ. Also, many millennials are having difficulty with folks receiving their prophetic words even though they are from Jesus. The verse 1 Timothy 4:12 will help explain why this is happening to this important body of believers. Let no man despise thy youth—that is, do not act in such a manner that any shall despise you on account of your youth. Act as you are becoming a minister of the gospel in all things and in such a way that people will respect you as such, though you are young. It is clear from this that Timothy was then a young man, but his exact age there is no means of determining. Let's look at the illustrations noted in these verses of scripture:

1. That there was danger that, by the levity and indiscretion to which young prophets are so much exposed, the ministry might be regarded with contempt.

2. That it was possible that his deportment should be so grave, serious, and every way appropriate, that the ministry would not be blamed, but honored. The "way" in which Timothy was to live so that the ministry would not be despised on account of his youth, the apostle proceeds immediately to specify.

But be thou an example of the believers. One of the constant duties of a minister of the gospel, no matter what his age. A millennial prophet should live so that if all his people should closely follow his example, their salvation would be secure, and they would make the highest possible attainments in piety. On the meaning of the word rendered "example," see the notes on Philippians 3:17; 1 Thessalonians 1:7.

In word - In "speech," that is, your manner of conversation. This does not refer to his "public teaching," in which he could not probably be an "example" to them, but to his usual and familiar conversation.

In conversation - In general deportment. See this word explained in the notes on Philippians 1:27.

In charity - Love to the brethren, and to all; see notes on 1 Corinthians 13.

In spirit - In the government of your passions, and in a mild, meek, forgiving disposition.

In faith - At all times, and in all trials show to believers by your example, how they ought to maintain unshaken confidence in God.

In purity - In chasteness of life; see 1 Timothy 5:2. There should be nothing in your contact with the other sex that would give rise to scandal. The papists, with great impropriety, understand this as enjoining celibacy, as if there could be no "purity" in that holy relation which God appointed in

Eden and which he has declared to "be honorable in all," Hebrews 13:4, and which he has made so essential to the wellbeing of mankind.

Finally, if the apostle had wished to produce the highest-possible degree of corruption in the church, he would have enjoined the celibacy of the clergy and the celibacy of an indefinite number of nuns and monks. There are no other institutions on the earth that have done so much to corrupt the chastity of the race as those which have grown out of the doctrine that celibacy is being an example for other young prophets to adhere to. The millennial prophet must be one that all can respect regardless of their age but can produce a standard by which everyone can measure their walk with the Lord.

Chapter 8
Selective Hearing (Adjustments)

Millennials also have this function in their spirit-man with their spirit-ears. They also have that function of selective hearing, and the way it works is that they tend to block out what millennials deem to be unimportant. You need something from the Lord, or maybe you want to talk with God, or maybe you are making a decision that you would really like the Lord's input on before you make that decision. So you go into the prayer closet, and you begin to pray. You tell God about your issue and say, "Lord, would you please speak to me?"

We are not exactly sure what we are waiting for, but we are waiting. We do not really know what we expect to hear. Nothing happens. So then we get a little more serious. We say, "Man, I better get my white handkerchief out because that's a little more serious. Man, we have a little white hanky in your hand, God's doing something now."

We really begin to pray and walk the floor and kind of foam at the mouth, and we are getting a hold of God now. We wait, and we do not hear anything. So all right, this is a serious one. I am going to lie on the floor, just lie prostrate before the Lord. You know, kick, scream, beg, plead, cajole. You know, whatever I have to do to get an answer from God. Finally, we are irritated, frustrated, stomp out of the prayer closet, and say God did not speak to me.

Have any of you millennials had an experience like that? It's frustrating, isn't it? God, why aren't you talking to me?

Well, what is happening is that we are listening to the Lord, but we have selective hearing. We are saying, "Okay, Lord, what do you have to say?" Then God says something to us, he whispers something into our heart, but we do not know what the voice of the Lord sounds like, so we do not recognize this as being God. We think it's some random noise or some sort of distraction. We may think our mind is wandering. We have such a hard time concentrating and focusing when praying. So we say to our mind, "Be quiet. I am trying to hear from God," and we set it aside. "Lord, speak to me!"

I can only imagine how God knits his eyebrows and says, "But I just talked to you."

"Lord, I just asked you. Please tell me what you want me to do in this situation."

He says, "Okay, here's what I want you to do . . ."

We say, "I am trying to hear from the Lord, be quiet."

Then we pound on the floor, we beg, we plead. God is saying, "Here's what you need to do . . .," and we are just so irritated and frustrated. So finally, we stomp out saying God did not talk to me.

What has really happened is that the Lord has spoken to us, but because we are not familiar with his voice and we do not recognize his voice, we do not know that it's God talking. Our selective hearing blocks it out, and we never realize that we have heard. We were hearing. We just did not know we were hearing.

This is good news. You can smile at this. Because you are already well down the road, you are already receiving God's input. All we have to do now is recognize it. Let me explain it to you this way: How many of you know identical twins—two siblings, born at the same time, and they look just alike? I have some very dear friends, Sam and Samuel, who are identical twins. These guys are millennials. They are such wonderful men, and I have enjoyed their company, but Sam and I have had a chance to pursue a special relationship.

I have known other twins besides them, and identical twins look just alike that you cannot tell them apart when you first meet them. There are no identifying mark, they are so alike in appearance. But a lot of times there can be an identifying mark that makes it easier to tell them apart. Sam and Samuel are like that.

When I first met them, their only identifying mark was a mustache. Sam had a mustache. Samuel, the one I got to know, did not have one. I got to know Sam but not quite as well. So that was the way that I told them apart.

I remember that I was invited to the church that they attended to speak. I had been to the church several times before. I was familiar with the pastor and elders and enjoyed being with them. The pastor spoke to me on the phone, and he said, "Why don't you drive up on Saturday and just drive up to one of the elder's houses?" He told me which elder. "They'll have dinner there, and you will have a little get-together with some of the elders and have a nice fellowship time." The pastor said he had other responsibilities that night, and that was okay because we had a good relationship. The pastor said, "Of course, you can come minister Sunday morning in the church."

Now I was expecting Samuel to be at this meeting, but Sam, the one with mustache, was not going to be able to make it. We drove up to the elder's house, and we knocked on the door, and Samuel answered the door, or was it Sam? I was faced with a bit of a dilemma. You see, I was expecting Samuel, and the man who answered the door did not have a mustache, so that means it was Sam. When I looked at him, I thought maybe it was Sam, but Sam was not supposed to be there, and this guy did not have a mustache. I was confused. Now this was a bit of an embarrassing moment when you have bonded with a man, and I had shared my heart with Samuel. I have told him things that I do not tell a lot of people. It's embarrassing when you are looking at a guy you shared your heart with and you do not even know if that's him. I am sure that they are used to it, but I am not. I am not a twin. I do not live this way. So I looked at this guy, and I just made an instantaneous decision that it must be Sam, even though this guy was clean-shaven. So I said, "Sam, how are you?"

"Good, Billy! Good to see you," Sam said.

Thank God, I was right. Sam had shaved off his mustache and had not told me. For some reason, he was there when he was not supposed to be there. This was so exciting to be able to recognize for who he really was. You are at a point where though they are identical, you are close enough to them that you can tell them apart.

Now on the inside of you, you have twins: one is the voice of the Lord, and one is the voice of your own heart. They are not the same. They are two separate things, but when you first learn to hear the voice of the Lord, they are like identical twins, and you cannot tell them apart. That's why you find yourself saying, "Is it me, or is it God?" You may think God's speaking to you, but you are not sure. "Pastor, this is what is going on in my life, and I am not sure if the Lord is speaking to me. I think so, but I am not sure."

You are looking at the twins, and you cannot tell them apart. Is it me, or is it God? Have you ever had that experience? Is this the voice of the Lord or the voice of my own heart? Now here's the way it works: When we were talking about this teaching, I asked Samuel if he could ever fool his mom and dad? Samuel said, "Well, maybe if I stood at the end of the hall with the lights out and my back turned and I did not say anything, I might be able to fool her for a moment. But other than that, there is no fooling Mom and Dad."

They can tell the twins apart. Why is that? Because they know them, they are familiar with them, they spent time with them. Those of you who have known identical twins know that the more time you spend with them, the more you recognize that they are actually two separate, distinct individuals, and it becomes very easy to tell them apart, doesn't it? Finally, you can even lose track of the fact that they are even twins. They just don't look alike anymore because you know them so well.

I was in Samuel's kitchen, and our family was staying with their family. We're just that close. His wife Janice was in the kitchen cooking. The kitchen, for me, is the meeting place in the house. It has a nice, warm, comfortable feel, especially when there is food on the stove. That's a good place to be. I was sitting on a stool in the kitchen, and Samuel was helping Janice, and my wife Shera was in and out. We were all just having a fun time of fellowship. I looked up at Samuel, and I had this dawning realization looking at his profile. Before I really had time to think, I said, "Samuel, you know, you and Sam look alike."

Duh, they're twins, identical twins. But I had become so familiar with Samuel and had known him well enough that I had lost track of the fact that they even looked alike. They were two separate people to me, and it was like a new, fresh, dawning realization that these two men even looked alike. That's how comfortable you can be with the twins.

That's how it is with the voice of the Lord and the voice of your own heart. God wants to bring you to the place where you can tell the voice of the Lord apart from your own heart, though they are twins, when you spend time listening to God, when you practice hearing the voice of the Lord in your everyday life, when you are constantly attuned to his voice, when you finally learn to recognize it, and we will be talking about that tonight. What does the voice of the Lord sound like? Give me a few identifiers so I can tell these twins apart. Describe the voice of the Lord so I can separate it from the voice of my own heart. When that finally happens, and you begin to listen regularly and consistently, a growing confidence comes. Pretty soon, the voice of the Lord and the voice of your own heart are two very separate distinct voices, and you can say, "This is me, and this is God."

Now I am not bragging, but I know when it is God and when it is me. This is what the Lord is saying. There is confidence there. That's where God wants us to be. He wants us to have that kind of confidence hearing him.

Many millennials are having a hard time processing which voice it is. Turn to Hebrews 5:14. This process of hearing the voice of the Lord is a learning process. It doesn't just happen overnight. We mentioned in our last teaching that it would be really nice if I could just come to you and lay hands on you or pray over you, and suddenly, you would just hear the voice of the Lord. It just doesn't happen that way. It's not just an impartation. That may play a role in it, but that is not primarily what it is. There is a learning process. Hebrews 5:14 says, "Strong meat belongs to them that are of full age. Even those that by reason of use have their senses exercised to discern both good and evil." Hearing the voice of the Lord is a learning process. It says, "Having their senses exercised to discern both good and evil." Your spiritual senses need to be exercised. They need to be developed, and it's by reason of use. It's a learning process, a developing process. It doesn't happen all at once or overnight. You don't go to the health spa and just come out looking great. It comes by using your muscles that they develop. Now let's look at what it says in the New International Version of the Bible. It says, "But solid food is for the mature, who by constant use have trained themselves to distinguish well from evil." Your spiritual senses need to be constantly used so that you can train yourself. You have got to work with the twins, spend time with the twins. You've got to spend time hearing the voice of the Lord. When you do that, your spiritual ears and eyes will become much more keen and sharper. You learn progressively by constant use. The Amplified Version of the Bible says this: "But solid food is for full grown men. For those whose senses and mental faculties are trained by practice to discriminate and distinguish between what is morally good and noble, what is evil and contrary either to divine and human law." It says they are trained by practice. That doesn't sound spiritual. You mean you have to practice hearing God? That's exactly what you have to do. You have to by constant use, and by progressive practice, we have to do it. Finally, this is something that many millennials struggle with daily because they want everything to go their way or the highway. Millennials do learn to differentiate which twin is talking to you!

Chapter 9
Stop, Jump, and Roll (Differences)

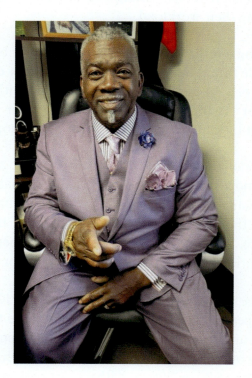

Amillennial is an individual reaching young adulthood in the early twenty-first century. These individuals typically fall within the years 1981–1996, which are aged twenty-three to thirty-eight in 2019. The millennial generation is also known as generation Y. This generation is the most tech savvy, meaning they are proficient with understanding technology. People in gen Y are usually hardworking as well. The main personality traits for millennials are friendly, reliable, easygoing, and down-to-earth.

The typical life of a millennial varies upon everyone. This begins from waking up in the morning, going to work or college, hanging out with friends or studying for that exam that is in three days, and ending the day by preparing for the next one. The millennial lifestyle is about living in a free and open society where our opportunities are above and beyond our expectations. Millennials struggle more with depression in today's time brought about by being exposed to higher stress in the workplace. One way millennials cope with depression is taking a vacation day from work to spend time on taking care of themselves and limiting their workload.

There are a lot of pros to being a millennial, but the major pro to being a millennial is that we can multitask—we can do multiple things at once. Millennials at work or college shine at multitasking. Millennials can study and work on big projects while talking with their friends. Around 37% of millennials would spend their break time scrolling through their social media feed to chat with colleagues. Being able to multitask helps millennials with being more productive.

Now with eating habits, 93% of millennials will choose takeout at least once a week. There are millennials that eat takeout more than once a week, but this probability is a lot lower. Considering takeout, most millennials usually spend around the average amount of money a week on takeout. Now if the millennials have their own family, then the amount they spend will be a lot higher, depending on their food choice. From a personal experience, one spent almost $20 a week on takeout, which is around the average price spent on takeout for the week for an individual.

With sleep times, mainly 36% of millennials go to bed between 10:00 and 11:00 PM on a national average. There are a smaller percentage of millennials that choose to go to bed before 9:00 PM. The average American gets 6.8 hours of sleep per night. Millennials usually sleep about 9 hours a night compared with 8.6 hours from other generations. Some millennials have the energy where they can go to bed at 12:00 AM and wake up at 6:00 or 7:00 AM with a lot of energy and ready to start the day again.

While the name generation Z seems to be the most widespread, they are also referred to as the selfie generation, post-millennials, and the trans generation. But regardless of the title, there are many things that differ millennials from generation Y. While millennials grew up in a technologically-savvy and connected world, younger members of gen Z cannot remember a world without the Internet. They grew up swiping an iPad before they learned how to talk and are the first generation to be raised in the era of smartphones. Teenage members of gen Z are connected nearly every waking hour of the day. Gen Z millennials have been raised with businesses such as Uber and Airbnb, seeing how easy and simple it is to use your own time and resources to make money. About 72% of older members of gen Z want to start their own business. They just don't have the patience to be ordered around throughout the day. They believe that being their own boss is more conductive and will produce the salary that is expected in this lifetime. They just need to and have to process more than any other millennials or gen Y.

This is the last generation that will be majority white (52%). Between 2000 and 2010, the country's Hispanic population grew at four times the rate of the total population. The idea of a black president is not exceptional to them—it's normal. Gen Zs have grown up experiencing diversity, and they feel overwhelmingly positive about it. In 1966, 6.6% of incoming freshmen reported being unaffiliated with any religion. In 2015, nearly one third (29.6%) of all incoming college students reported not identifying with any particular religion. The question is whether young people today are truly moving away from religion or just defining themselves differently than previous generations. I tend toward the latter explanation, although there is probably some truth in the first.

Formerly-distinct lines are now considered "blurry." Technology has blurred the lines between home and work, study and entertainment, and public and private. Gen Zs have a different experience of family— same-sex households, working moms, stay-at-home dads, three-parent families, and couples choosing not to have kids. The nuclear family will make up less than a third of all families by 2026. And of course, gender and romantic identities have become blurry as well. In her interviews with teens for her article in *Time* magazine, says that "there was a pervasive sense that being a teenager today is a draining full-time job that includes doing schoolwork, managing a social media identity and fretting about career, climate change, sexism, racism—you name it." About 68% feel overwhelmed by everything they need to do each week.

About 3 million adolescents, twelve to seventeen, have had a "major depressive episode" in the past year. There has been an increase in anxiety and depression among high school students since 2012. And this upsurge cuts across virtually all demographics—suburban, urban, and rural. Most gen Z plan to get married, have children, and buy a home, although probably later than previous generations. And they are less likely to drink, smoke, and take drugs. Yet they hold more progressive views on issues like the legality of marijuana and the morality of same-sex marriage. You must capture the forces that have helped create an individualistic emphasis among this generation: "Gen Z is used to having everything personalized just for them, from playlists to newsfeeds to products features of all kinds. They've grown up expecting that. There is a tendency to be either overly romantic or critical about new generations. The reality is that members of generation Z face the same life challenges as previous generations, but in a super-connected and rapid-moving technological age. And let us not forget that they have the same deep needs for love, significance, meaning, and belonging as every previous generation.

The next generation hungry to enter the workplace is generation Z. According to the U.S. Census Bureau, gen Z (the post-millennial generation) makes up 25% of the population. (Read this to learn more about generation Z.)

About 62% of generation Z anticipate challenges working with baby boomers and generation X; only 5% anticipate challenges working with millennials. Companies with a firm understanding of the expectations and preferences of the emerging generations will be well equipped to attract the next generation of talent, maximize their potential, alleviate the inevitable cross-generational challenges, and capitalize on cognitive diversity through a generationally-diverse workforce.

About 77% of generation Z expect to work harder than previous generations. Millennials became optimistic, thanks to their encouraging baby-boomer parents and growing up in a time of prosperity and opportunity. Gen Z will be realistic, thanks to their skeptical and straight-shooting generation X parents and growing up in a recession. According to Pew Charitable Trusts, during the Great Recession, the median net worth of gen Z's parents fell by nearly 45%.

About 71% of generation Z said they believe the phrase "If you want it done right, then do it yourself."

When given the option to arrange a group of desks, millennials would opt for a collaborative arrangement and assemble the desks into a circle. Generation Z will be more competitive with their colleagues and will harness a do-it-yourself mentality at work. In fact, 69% of gen Z would rather have their own workspace than share it with someone else.

About 40% of generation Z said that working Wi-Fi was more important to them than working bathrooms.

According to Pew Research, only 14% of U.S. adults had access to the internet in 1995, but by 2014, 87% had access. Millennials were pioneers in the digital age. They witnessed the introduction and rise of social media, instant messaging, smartphones, search engines, and the mobile revolution.

Generation Z did not witness these innovations, but rather, they were born into it. Ubiquitous connectivity, highly-curated global information, on-demand video, and 24/7 news cycles are native to gen Z.

About 70% of generation Z would rather share personal information with their pet than with their boss.

As digital pioneers, millennials explored, and in some cases exploited, social media and made public their thoughts, opinions, and every noteworthy or menial life update. With safety and security top of mind, generation Z will be much more calculated or selective with the information they share online. For example, gen Z gravitated to Snapchat because time-bound content doesn't live online forever like a tweet or Facebook post does.

About 74% of generation Z prefer to communicate face-to-face with colleagues.

Millennials pioneered many of the digital communication tools (texting, instant messaging, slack, etc.) that have made the workplace more efficient and effective, but some would argue less personable. Equipped with their experience communicating using full sight, sound, and motion over Skype, FaceTime, Snapchat, etc., generation Z is positioned as the ideal generation to finally strike the right balance between online and offline workplace communications.

About 75% of generation Z say there are other ways of getting a good education than going to college, according to Sparks & Honey.

Millennials are questioning if their large student debt was worth it, especially considering that 44% of recent college grads are employed in jobs not requiring degrees and one in eight recent college grads is unemployed. Generation Z will explore education alternatives. They will pursue on-demand or just-in-time learning solutions, like how-to YouTube tutorials, or will seek employers that offer robust on-the-job and development training.

About 75% of generation Z would be interested in a situation in which they could have multiple roles within one place of employment.

Growing up in fast times and coming of age in an on-demand culture, millennials have little patience for stagnation, especially when it comes to their careers. (Read this to learn how to cure millennials of their career impatience.) Generation Z won't want to miss out on any valuable experience and will want to flex their on-demand learning muscle by trying out various roles or projects (marketing, accounting, human resources, etc.) inside of the organization.

About 58% of adults, age thirty-five and over, worldwide agree that "kids today have more in common with their global peers than they do with adults in their own country."

Millennials were considered the first global generation because they shared similar characteristics and values across borders, and they were able to view significant global events in real time. However, generation Z interacts with their global peers with greater fluidity than any other generation. As more of the world comes online, geographies will continue to shrink, causing gen Z to view themselves as global citizens.

Chapter 10
Family Feud (Values)

Coping with Imprisonment of a Millennial Family Member

Prayer - Most Christian parents tend to forget that our prayer is a weapon and how powerful it is. Families that are in these types of situations need to realize that your faith is really going to be tried. It may even get to the point where you're forced to answer tough questions about what you believe and don't believe. Our God is the one and only true living God. He can reach down and touch places in your loved one's heart that you didn't even know existed. What's more, he has a way of doing this most effectively when the human heart is at its lowest: "The Lord is near to those who have a broken heart, and saves those such as having a contrite spirit" (Psalm 34:18). It's possible that your millennial is more open to the work of the Holy Spirit now than at any time in his life. This is the time to ask the Lord to bombard him with the message of Christ's forgiveness and love.

Visits - If the facility where your family member is incarcerated is not too far away, face-to-face visits from loved ones mean more to prisoners than most of us on the outside can easily grasp. If time is limited, it may help to write out what you want to say in advance. Then you can read it aloud at the time of your visit. A good rule of thumb to remember is this: Visit as much as possible during the time your family member is nearby. If they are relocated and moved further away, you may not get to visit them as much as you would like because of the distance.

Communication - The art of writing letters has been a major loss in our contemporary culture, but in a situation like this, where contact by phone, e-mail, or text message is out of the question, writing is a powerful motivation to rediscover it. A letter is an excellent way to express your thoughts with care and deliberation. This is exactly what's needed under the circumstances. To the prisoner on the receiving end, it's a beacon of light and hope from the outer world. So write regularly and often, at least once a week. Use the written word to reassure your loved one of your unconditional love.

There are over a million men and women in prison in the United States more than any other country in the world. That means a comparable number of mothers have children in prison. Incarceration affects so many others, such as family members, friends, fathers, sisters, brothers, grandparents, wives, husbands, and children. Unfortunately, sometimes it may even occur in the generation of our family. We don't like to talk about it because it's not something we are proud of, yet it's reality. It is not the first thing one mentions, nor maybe the last, when discussing family members. "Well, how are the kids doing?" You will hear about the one with the Bachelor of Science degree from Harvard who runs her own business, or the son who has his Master of Business Administration from the University of Wisconsin, or the son who is a scholar/athlete, but not always about the one in prison.

People aren't too reluctant to share that their child or family member is in prison. When your child makes a wrong turn, bad choice, breaks the law, the parents usually get the blame, or they blame themselves. It is quite natural, for example, when there is a serial killer that the news media will search out the person's background. What kind of mom did he/she have? Ask most parents who have children in prison, and they probably would have advised against the behavior that resulted in their children being incarcerated. However, now they are dealing with the consequences. Interestingly, however, when you mention to others that your family member is in prison, people will confide that their son or daughter is or was in prison, themselves were once incarcerated, or a friend's son was in prison. But it takes someone first to mention it, and obviously, one picks and chooses who to tell, especially keeping in mind that your child will face a lot of discrimination and hurdles upon release.

To begin with, it is with great anguish for a person to see their child or family member shackled and handcuffed in court. In addition, the first visit to the prison is a lesson in frustration: walk this path, no cell phones beyond this point, sign here, leave your driver's license there, make sure you read signs and follow all rules on the inside, etc. As a parent, one almost becomes a prisoner yourself. Added are the other hurdles to undergo, such as paying outrageous phone bills for a few calls, paying huge amounts for food that can be bought for much less outside the prison, not being able to phone, being worried about your family member being beat up or tasered, but most of all, being concerned about how they will cope with a prison environment and how their adjustment on the outside upon release.

Millennials Transitioning from High School to College

Upon graduating from high school, most millennial males and females are about ready to start college. In the day and age that we live in now, considered as the B2B generation, students are accustomed to working their way through school. More and more, traditional and adult learners are balancing their studies with full- or part-time work. In fact, it's been reported that about 70–80% of college students are active in the labor market while enrolled in college. Today's college students are feeling the strain of our busy modern world. In fact, 45% of college students said they experience "more than average stress," and 87% said they felt overwhelmed by all they had to do at least once in the previous year, according to the American College Health Association-2018 National College Health Assessment.

Many are nervous as they begin to think about the new environment they will be exposed to with new friends, new responsibilities, and new opportunities. This will be their new home for the next few years, or some of them may choose to live at home and commute back and forth to school. Transitioning from high school to college can be hard. With the help and encouragement from their local church, along with family, they will be equipped with the tools to push them to the limits that will enable them to be on the road of success for their future career. Friends that were made in high school may be going to different schools, but don't worry, that's just how life goes. They will be in a new environment, but don't fret, a good rule of thumb to follow is to try and get them to step out of their comfort zone. Just making one or two friends to join them in their first few weeks may completely change their experience during college to more of a comfort zone. Joining clubs and organizations that interest them is another way for them to step out of their comfort zone.

Freshman year is when nobody knows anyone, and it's the best time to get closer to classmates so you can have them with you during the next few years. There are just a few of our many schools that offer this program to freshmen students. On campus, students will have an opportunity to be with colleagues who share the same interests as them and get a chance to be closer with the community. The level of studying at college will be different and more concentrated from high school. The resources needed to get through this will vary quite a bit, from textbooks to computers and equipment. Having what you need to get through your classes is important but can be difficult to obtain and manage. Just know that there are ways to get help with them. Don't rush to buy any textbooks before the first day of classes. Find out whether those textbooks are needed for the class beforehand.

Many professors have a textbook that is required on their syllabus. However, sometimes you will not use the textbook during the course of your semester. If they are, there are ways to save money on them by acquiring used textbooks or the growing number. Also, be sure to take advantage of a professor's office hours. Chances are, if you are looking for ways to improve your grade, going to office hours is one of the suggestions always listed and can help you get the inside track on how to succeed in class.

Going to college is already an adjustment; it is easy to feel alone and filled with working on self-improvement. Encourage your son or daughter to not be intimidated by social media because when people feel insecure, it is easy to withdraw and substitute virtual relationships for real ones. Procrastination is a red flag that can stick its ugly head up. Procrastination creates a self-fulfilling prophecy because if your child waits until the last minute to do his work, the product will likely be lacking. Suggest breaking down the task into small manageable steps that can easily be completed.

There is a famous meme: A long journey always begins with small steps. Learning to problem solve is a very important coping skill. You teach your child to define problems so they aren't vague and he can come up with possible solutions. Recommend to your child to think about having a "plan B" in his head when he notes a problem since things don't always go the way you want or expect. This is the best time to become your child's best advocate in the upcoming years. A few assertiveness lessons wouldn't hurt at all.

Millennials Transitioning from Home to Military

Having a son or daughter head into the unknown can be a very unsettling experience. In your eyes, you probably still remember them running around the house wearing diapers. In the blink of an eye, they're walking out the door and heading to Basic Training. There's no doubt in your mind as to whether you are proud of your child's decision to enlist—that is quite obvious. The hard part for you is the fact that you are going to miss them being in your life on a daily basis. While it's hard to imagine those thoughts, life happens fast, but that doesn't mean that you have to try to process these thoughts and feelings on your own. There are millions of other parents who have gone through the very same thoughts and emotions as you. Instead of trying to work through them alone, why not reach out to other parents who may have some good insight and advice for you? If you know someone personally, that is great. Otherwise, you can ask friends and family members if they have anyone in mind whom you can talk to. It's very comforting knowing that you have someone to confide in instead of trying to process these thoughts and feelings on your own. Everyone loves a good party or a nice night out to dinner with their family. Why not send them off in style by planning a simple going-away party before leaving for Basic Training? It's the perfect way for your child to say goodbye to everyone while also displaying the awesome career path that they've chosen for their life. Don't be afraid to have fun with the details and include other family members and friends to help out in the planning. Load up the tables with your child's favorite foods and treats and spend the evening celebrating them and their accomplishments. Reach out to other parents who have been through these feelings and emotions before. This is an opportunity for you to listen to their stories related to questions or concerns that you may have.

So many parents automatically have the fear that they won't be able to talk to or hear from their child once they leave for basic training. That just isn't true. While the communication may be a bit less than what you want it to be, it can and will still happen. Remember that your millennial is starting out on a new venture in their life and is going to be tired and exhausted, so give them time to make their adjustments before worrying about when you are going to hear from them. Your main form of communication with your millennial during Basic Training is through letters and postcards. He or she should be able to call home throughout training, but these calls are generally limited to a maximum of one per week and, many times, are less often than that. Before they leave for Basic Training, accept that you will only hear from them through letters, and it will be much easier to deal with in the following weeks. Don't send mail until you get their mailing address. If you don't have the correct mailing address, it will go round and round in the postal system on post before getting to them, if it ever does. Be patient and wait for official notification of their correct mailing address before sending any mail.

While it's hard to imagine, those thoughts and feelings do get easier. The key to staying sane during the time that your millennial is gone at Basic Training is to stay busy and surround yourself with positivity. Picking up new hobbies for you is always a great idea during this time as well. Join a gym, a reading club, or spend your days outdoors in the garden. There are many kinds of activities that will help ease your mind while still doing something that you enjoy can be a huge help!

When your millennial leaves for Basic Training, hold your head up! This is just a taste of the wonderful things that are going to transpire for them, and you get to be the proud parent on the sidelines cheering them along the entire way! Stay attentive, stay positive, and stay supportive, and you'll find that the time that they are gone for Basic Training will be over quickly! The very moment you receive their graduation date, go ahead and start planning. Make sure you book your hotel room ahead of time and flight schedules are all taken care of so that when it's time for you to leave, your mind will be free of stress. Many boot camp graduates might just want to spend much of their time relaxing in the hotel room because they have spent weeks and weeks in a very structured and stressful environment. It's simply all right, you're there to show your love and moral support.

Get prepared to stay in touch when you find out where they are going to be stationed at. Keep your phone with you at all times because you don't want to miss any calls. Your computer will be one of your closest friends or mostly everyone uses their Facebook Messenger to FaceTime their friends and loved ones. Make sure yours is updated! This will be very valuable to see your millennial's face and talk with him or her, especially if they receive orders to go overseas and may not be traveling home for quite some time. This will ease your mind and heart to be able to communicate with them and to know that they are doing well. Be prepared to count down the days when the holidays are approaching to spend the endless days with them when they travel home to visit you from whatever location they are stationed. You will want to enjoy every moment of time that you have with them because these are the precious memories that you will treasure forever.

A common misconception of millennials is that they are lazy and incompetent. Millennials tend to be well versed in the constantly-changing world of technology. They're open to change and meet problems head on. They do not fear obstacles and, instead, get excited about the opportunities that obstacles may create. I believe that we can learn a lot from this generation if we keep an open mind to do so.

Although millennials are just ordinary individuals like the rest of us in society, they value positive reinforcement and take pride in knowing that they have completed a task with quality and purpose. A good recommendation is to always keep an open-door policy with your millennial. This is the biggest encouragement for them that reaches far above money or fame because they want a sense of purpose and accomplishment.

Chapter 11
The War Within

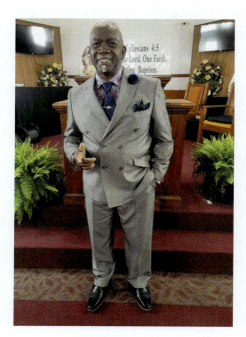

Most people go their lives unaware of this invisible enemy. It's a kind of hidden realm past the normal senses that many don't understand how to cope with. You see right now you're probably carrying at least a little emotional baggage on your shoulders, things like fear, worries, and doubts. It's all part of living a humanistic life. Most folks are not just lugging around a little baggage, but it is buried under it. This mind system will cause you to awake every morning feeling how most people do at the end of the day, i.e., drained, exhausted, and overwhelmed. Millennials seem to feel alone, helpless, and overtaken by anxiety. Most just want to crawl up in a shell and hide from the world like a turtle that has been startled. To make matters worse, many are in college, and their finances are about to crush them alive. The anxiety chokes the very life out of you, and you feel like giving up and quitting in the game of life. To make matters worse still, many are facing Mount Everest-size debt.

The war within of having student loan debt will cause you to toss and turn endlessly every night, worrying, "How am I going to cover this month's minimum payments and still have money for the light bill?" Many millennials have already declared bankruptcy before age thirty because of the responsibilities associated with being a college student pursuing a degree. Looking back, I can definitely say my life was not what I wanted it to be, but like most people, maybe where you are right now, life can be difficult and not perfect and many galaxies away from what you once hoped for. The problem is somewhere along your path, you get stuck in the quicksand, and now every move pulls you deeper into the bottomless pit. Many have tried self-help books and courses, practiced meditation, yoga, and maybe even given therapy a try. As the years pass, you are still dealing with the same heartbreaking money challenges, the same depilatory health problems, and the same old traumas you've carried since childhood. Many cannot help but wonder if this is it. *I am doomed to live out the same old problems for the rest of my life.*

Over the centuries, many mystics, poets, and storytellers have given this experience many names. The name that sticks out like a sore thumb is the war within. Even though you may not have heard this phrase, chances are you have felt the darkness. Maybe you're feeling it at this moment. It's why you are reading this book today. I didn't know about any shortcuts, and the darkness felt as though a category 5 hurricane was locked in my head. There were nights I found myself struggling to fall asleep, and when I did, horrifying dreams shook me back awake, and then my legs and feet just sort of stopped working. I developed a mysterious condition where I had trouble walking around the block without excruciating pain. Test after test, doctor after doctor, and it reveals no answer. But now it was like I was a thirty-years-old caged in the body of an octopus. The physical toll was a breeze compared to the whirlwind unleashed inside. Many millennials and generation Z experience what I call the bleed out as old emotional wounds begin to haunt them as they reach into the future and decide if this is really what and who they want to be. If this is happening to you, then it's not that you are going crazy, but you are being introduced to your old attachments from your childhood, and you wonder, *Should I unleash or hold on to these feelings and anxieties?*

This war in the mind will begin to rage war with you if you do not address the issues at hand, i.e., mistakes made when you were a teenager, bad decisions about what college to attend, and finally, who you feel in love with. Many find themselves crying like a newborn baby and end up curling up in a ball as the flow of tears rush down their cheeks. There was so much unprocessed garbage, and you will begin to feel everything. Truly, can you relate to any of this? I think we have all been there at least once in our short lifespan. What if there was a secret button to turn even the deepest nightmare into the brightest daylight? Would you simply push it once, twice, or how many times would you have used it, my friend?

Time management is the most valuable asset because one's performance shall be a direct measure of how wisely one invests one's time. A lot of millennials say, "I just do not have the time to invest in finishing college because I have bills that need to be paid. I now have a family and a young child to take care of. Where is the time to do anything else?" The war will continue to rage unless you get a hold on Mr. Time. Here are a few suggestions that helped me while I was in college and making decisions on what directions to take in life. One may say that life is not easy, and the correct answer is yes, that is so true. However, the dichotomy of it all makes for a very interesting theory about how you can get caught up in the trade winds of life. These winds will suck you in unless you have the 5P plan at your disposal. What is the 5P plan, someone is now asking. It's a war, and I understand the fight you are in because I have been there before, and trust me, it was scary! The 5P plan is simply this: *prior planning prevents poor performance*. Question no. 1: Do you have a plan of excursion? Here are my suggestions:

1.   Developing Time Management Skills

It is all about being ahead of other competing aspirants. An aspirant who manages his/her schedule well takes a leap with an edge over the competitors. Developing time management skills demand the following four critical things to be executed:

- Prioritizing the assignments
- Making an effective schedule
- Creating blocks of study time
- Avoiding procrastination and distraction

Every aspirant must achieve the plan and execute these four aspects of time management to crack with a good All India Rank so that they can get into the college of their choice.

2.   Concentrate on High-Priority Chapters of Each Subject

The quickest and most effective way of increasing productivity for anyone is to spend time on things that advance their productivity substantially in 2021. Some chapters, historically, have always had more weightage. Students should prioritize the preparation of such chapters and make the most out of them so that maximum questions can be easily attempted correctly in 2021.

Such chapters from each subject are shown graphically for your better understanding and preparation.

3. Exercise Self-Discipline

Self-discipline enables one to stay focused on a task and work on it until it is completed. Once they have established their priorities, they should refuse to let distractions, interruptions, or happenings of the moment destroy their concentration. Allotting a specific number of hours to each chapter and then completing them in a given time without getting distracted is how one can develop discipline.

Post finishing a chapter, students should practice relevant questions in a given frame of time. Every mistake committed while solving the topic based questions must be revisited and re-revised to refrain from repeating the same in the future.

4. Be Persistent

Careful planning and goal setting, determination to achieve, and recognizing the benefits of reaching a goal are essential to accomplish the targets students have assigned for themselves. This combination of factors enables one to be persistent. Many millennials eagerly take on a new plan of preparation, starting with a great splash and making quick progress, but they soon lose momentum, never executing the plan completely.

So to get the desired outcome of every plan, millennials and generation Z should be persistent and driven by the predefined timeline and finish the task per the plan, keeping the 5P plan in mind.

5. Get Started Now

The best way to guarantee completion of a task is to get started on it—now. Two reasons account for failure: either one never starts or one never finishes.

Following these guidelines will enable you to avoid these procrastination pitfalls:

- Millennials should begin the task and continue working on it even if they don't feel like it. Getting started is often the most difficult part of any task or plan; once begun, "inspiration" often follows.

- Generation Z students need to ace the fact that some chapters or assignments or tests will never be "easy," now or later. Getting started with chapters or assignments per the plan and working systematically to complete them will enable students to enjoy a sense of mastery and also boost their confidence.

Additionally, students should not refer to any random books available with them, keeping in mind that time management is essential, keeping the wars of the mind, body, and soul at bay. It's also a great feeling to know that your house is in order. Order is something that many don't understand that this starts as a child.

We learn this method from childhood by simply learning how to pay attention. This will not only familiarize them with the exam pattern but also with the types of questions asked, difficulty level, etc. Along with that, students can evaluate their preparation level, determine the time spent on each question, and accordingly work on their speed and accuracy.

Paying Attention to Other People

According to psychologist Simon Baron-Cohen, attention is one of the first underlying precursors to the development of a fully-fledged theory of mind.

This involves recognizing that seeing is not merely looking, but rather, we can selectively direct our attention to specific objects and people (Baron-Cohen, 1991). A key example of this attention is joint attention.

Joint attention occurs when two people direct their attention towards the same thing of interest, often doing via pointing so as to direct another's attention to the same source.

When infants understand this gesture, they are simultaneously processing another person's mental state, recognizing that this object is something that another person thinks is of interest (Baron-Cohen, 1991), thus illustrating the beginning phases of the theory of mind.

Intentionality (Knowing That People Act According to the Things They Want)

A second core component that contributes to the development of the theory of mind is that of intentionality or the understanding that others' actions are goal-directed and arise out of unique beliefs and desires as defined by philosopher Daniel Dennett (1983).

Toddlers as young as two years old exhibit an understanding of intentionality (Luchkina et al., 2018) as do chimpanzees and orangutans (Call and Tomas Ello, 1998).

To understand that people act in a way that is motivated by their desires (for example, I am hungry, so I will reach for that apple) is to understand that other people have their own desires (she must be hungry), thus demonstrating a theory of mind or attributing mental states to others.

Imitation (Copying Other People)

Imitating others is a third building block of theory of mind. The ability to imitate others is to recognize that others have their own beliefs and desires.

For example, bridging attention and intentionality, imitation can result when a child realizes that others direct their attention (to an object, etc.) and do so intentionally (motivated by goal-directed behavior). Internalizing these two concepts, the child then engages in imitation and may direct his or her eyes towards that specific object or scene. However, there is some pushback that imitation is not as much of a crucial precursor for theory of mind. A 2000 longitudinal study found that the infants' imitation scores were not associated with later theory of mind ability (Charman, 2000).

Stages of Theory of Mind

Between ages four and five, children really start to think about others' thoughts and feelings, and this is when true theory of mind emerges. The actual development of the theory of mind generally follows an agreed-upon sequence of steps (Wellman, 2004; Wellman and Peterson, 2012):

Tasks Listed from Easiest to Most Difficult

- Understanding "wanting": The first step is the realization that others have diverse desires, and to get what they want, people act in different ways.
- Understanding "thinking": The second step is the understanding that others also have diverse beliefs about the same thing and that people's actions are based on what they think is going to happen.

- Understanding that "seeing leads to knowing": The third stage is recognizing that others have different knowledge access, and if someone hasn't seen something, they will need extra information to understand.

- Understanding "false beliefs": The fourth stage is being aware of the fact that others may have false beliefs that differ from reality.

- Understanding "hidden feelings": The final stage is being aware that other people can hide their emotions and can feel a different emotion from the one they display.

Cultural Differences

While these developmental stages seem to be universal across demographic groups in laying the groundwork for the formation of theory of mind, different cultures place varying levels of emphasis on each of the five skills, causing some to be developed later than others. In other words, cultural importance plays a role in determining the specific order in which these five milestones are cemented into the mind of a toddler. That is, those that are more valued tend to be developed before those that are less so, and this makes sense from an evolutionary perspective too. For example, in individualistic cultures, such as the United States, a greater emphasis is placed on the ability to recognize that others have different opinions and beliefs. However, in more collectivistic cultures, such as China, this skill is not as valued and, as a result, might not develop until the war of the mind has been diminished by focusing on what abilities do I really have to offer. The war is real, and life must go on.

Chapter 12
That's a Fact, Jack (Points)

Most millennial consumers are immune to traditional advertisements. Statistics say that around 57% of millennials compare prices in stores, especially the malls. This is so amazing that 50% of all bloggers are millennials. Also, to add talent to consumption, 41% of millennials have no landline at home and rely on their cellphones to lead, guide, and show them everything they need to do and say. Millennials participate 77% of the time in loyalty reward programs that can generate them some sort of income or discounts. Most millennials do not want their managers telling them what to do, and the percentage is around 41%. Millennials make most of their purchases using a smartphone, and this too is around 41%. This is great news to hear that more than a quarter of millennials (27%) are already self-employed because it's just not feasible to work for someone else for minimal wages now. The voting of most millennials are influenced by their parents 48% of the time, and this happens because they have heard all about politics while they were home with family. Millennials in the United States wield about $1.3 trillion in annual revenue and buying power.

Most millennials will stay on a job they love 64% of the time if they are making 40,000 or more. They will not work for nothing like their parents did to support a family because they want all the advanced equipment to use with their social media devices. The future voting electorate will be led by over 40% of the millennial population. The millennial population of about 87% of online adults use Facebook. This ranges from the ages of eighteen to twenty-nine years old. The new movement that will usher in the greenhouse effect will be this millennial generation because they care about the environment. Social media is one of the strong areas that millennials connect with U.S. companies for a job opportunity. This percentage is about five out of six millennials. The millennial world participates about 54% of the time in wanting to start a business or already have one started. The student loan syndrome has caused millennials to carry a total of about $1 trillion in student debt. Millennials are the most racially-diverse generation and have no problems with what folks believe or who they love. Newsflash, a third of U.S. adults, eighteen to thirty-four, live at home with their parents, and 45% believe a decent-paying job is a privilege not a right. Millennials are earning 20% less than their parents.

There are about 22 million millennial parents in the United States. Also, millennials value community, family, and creativity in their work. They are more tolerant of different races and groups than older generations. The spending rate of millennials is expected to be about $3.45 trillion. Millennials are on track to become the most educated generation, and just eight in ten millennials have jobs, and some are even part time. Millennials think and believe that about 44% of marriages will become obsolete. Nearly a third have put off marriage or having a baby because of this recession and pandemic. Many millennials, around 50%, believe that Social Security will not exist when they reach retirement age. Also, about half of the cohabiting-couple households are headed by millennials.

Millennials are the most technological people and the smartest because everything is at their disposal. Millennials multitask better than anyone else. They have learned how to eat the fish and spit out the bones. They are able to walk and chew gum at the same time. They are codependent and need more than most other folks. The parents have created the millennials that need more than most. Most are depressed because they cannot cope with the situation at hand, i.e., I do not have any Jordans to wear, so I cannot go to the mall today. The reasoning behind this failed parenting is that most homes don't have both parents there to help balance them as they were growing up. Millennial parenting is not the same as it used to be. They do not practice family time, so the children want everything they see, and most are having sex before they get married. They also believe that cohabitation is better so you can get to know your partner, and many believe this will alleviate so much divorce.

Millennials are now twenty-five to forty years old and are heavily in debt, more than any age group before them. They are much "broker" than their parents and older cousins. Bloomberg analysis found that millennials are worse off financially than any generation before them. Financial experts say many graduated from college at an unfortunate time. Just as the government was coming into its Great Recession, many millennials were finding that jobs were not as plentiful as when they first entered college, and their student loan debt, which they may have amassed, was larger than any previous generation. The student loan just wasn't easy to pay back. Financial experts say there's a popular saying that millennials want the best, and they want it right now. They think, with easily-available credit, they can easily get the best. Many millennials have tied themselves to a debt cycle that's hard to recover from. That's not the freedom we are told that millennials are wanting.

Financial experts say student loans and buying top-of-the-line items with credit cards is crippling them. Low interest rates combined with the availability of credit has allowed many millennials to continue to accumulate amassed debt and not attack their student loan debt or even pay down their credit cards. He says many graduated college during the Great Recession years with the largest student loans ever seen in the United States.

Millennials have a lot of technical issues, such as the body being weakened to heavy work, but the mind is strong because of the educational skills they have. They are very impatient and got to have it right now. Generation X believes that hard work breeds success. A millennial's attitude is "today only." So much is available to millennials, and a galaxy is at their disposal. They have the most mental issues, and they have accepted everyone's appearance. Most millennials are not leaders but followers, and they are very smart.

Millennials have four factual points that most people do not think they process. However, trial and error has caused them to man and woman up in these critical areas of life. I want to share with you briefly the four L words that they have learned down through the years as millennials. Brace yourself as you read these next few verses because many millennials really did not want to have these responsibilities. Many have always relied on someone else to be the trailblazer for them. This generation of Y and Z has revolutionized the word "mantra." Millennials need a lot of motivation to get rid of the what-if and if-only scenarios. The mantra avoids laziness, pointless activities, and the neglect of responsibilities.

Millennials are often daydreamers who spend a lot of time during awake hours imagining how things in life could be. Many millennials have learned how to discern the wisest decision when faced with making the right choice. Let's get right into what many have developed from reading and social media events.

Leadership is essential. Family members, usually the adults, must assume responsibility for leading the family. If no one accepts this vital role, the family will weaken. Each family needs its own special set of rules and guidelines. These rules are based on the family member's greatest understanding of one another, not forces. The guidelines pass along from the adults to the children by example, with firmness and fairness. Strong families can work together to establish their way of life, allowing children to have a voice in decision-making and enforcing rules. However, in the initial stages and in times of crisis, adult family members must get the family to work together.

Next, we have *loyalty*. Strong families have a sense of loyalty and devotion toward family members. The family sticks together. They stand by one another during times of trouble. They stand up for one another when attacked by someone outside the family. Loyalty builds through sickness and health, want and good fortune, failure and success, and all the things the family faces. The family is a place of shelter for individual family members. In times of personal success or defeat, the family becomes a cheering section or a mourning bench. They also learn a sense of give and take in the family, which helps prepare them for the necessary negotiation in other relationships.

Love is at the heart of the family. All humans have the need to love and to be loved, and the family is normally the place where love is expressed. Love is the close personal blending of physical and mental togetherness. It includes privacy, intimacy, sharing, belonging, and caring. The atmosphere of real love is one of honesty, understanding, patience, and forgiveness. Such love does not happen automatically, it requires constant daily effort by each family member. Loving families share activities and express a great deal of gratitude for one another. Love takes time, affection, and a positive attitude.

Laughter is good family medicine. Humor is an escape valve for family tension. Through laughter, we learn to see ourselves honestly and objectively. Building a strong family is serious business, but if taken too seriously, family life can become very tense. Laughter balances our efforts and gives a realistic view of things. To be helpful, family laughter must be positive in nature. Laughing together builds up a family. Laughing at one another divides a family. Families that learn to use laughter in a positive way can release tensions, gain a clearer view, and bond relationships.

Printed in the United States
by Baker & Taylor Publisher Services